SEPTEMBER ROSES

SEPTEMBER ROSES

THOMAS ERWIN WELLS

DEDICATION

September Roses is dedicated to Mrs. Beverly Graham, my seventh-grade English teacher.
Even though she tried her best to teach me how to conjugate a verb, I was more interested in how she could work a skirt and the click of her heels.
That woman wasn't no pushover... she could swing a paddle like nobody's business!
After all these years, we're still friends on Facebook.
Beverly Graham will always be an inspiration to me.
Thank you, Mrs. Graham!

PREFACE

Hi! My name is Joe. Have you ever seen a September Rose? You probably have, but just didn't pay much attention. I didn't either, not until Morilla. You see, a September Rose is just like the roses of Spring... And Summer. They're decidedly not as vibrant, as they lack the vitality of youth. Though their pedals are faded, and slightly singed around the edges, they still have within the heart of them, redeeming qualities.

September Roses have stood the test of time. They are the ones who long to be gently plucked and given freely, like a lover's kiss. To be placed on love's alter as a sacrifice... their destiny fulfilled. To be pillaged and plundered as a sacrament to love's joy and sorrow. For you see, between two hearts, one will be left to mourn. It will be the mourner's Soul that will rise in gladness, for the two again shall be as one. And so it was to be for Morilla and me, in the Autumn of our lives. Like... "September Roses."

CHAPTER
ONE

I retired at sixty-two, knowing well that early retirement would cut my social security benefits by almost a third. However, working three more years in a world that for me had lost its texture, its color, and for the most part its flavor, seemed to me in a single word, futile.

The rest of my life, or so I thought at that time, would be a never-ending procession of decrepitation until the day came that I would wake up in the afterlife dead as a door nail. Not from some dread disease would I die, but simply to escape from the impetuous boredom of living. I thought it inevitable that one day my heart would just stop beating. The coroner would not attribute my demise, to any reason in particular, for none would be accountable other than a complete and utter lack of interest in pursuing this bad joke... this bum rap called, life.

I was convinced that my toil and struggle would not so much as leave a telltale sign on the world. The fact that I had come, or gone, or even passed this way, was without significance. I was resigned to watching my garden wilt and the fruit therein come to spoilage. Then be consumed by worms and rot, then returned to the soil from whence my flesh had come.

By my 63rd year, I had completely given up on the human race. I had no desire for friendship. Life had given me enough of my own crow to eat, without being a sad sack over someone else's troubles. At best, I had only a few acquaintances. Most of them were from down at the little neighborhood store where I bought beer. I would exchange an occasional smile there with the old men playing dominoes on the stoop. Misery loves company because company is where life hides its last ray of hope. Goodness be to mercy, those ole Black men on the stoop playing dominoes, are likely why I'm still above ground.

I ended up in New Orleans after my last failed business venture. The only thing the Pizza Biz had succeeded in doing, was taking the last breath of wind I had left right out of my sails. I was cast on the ocean of life like a ship without a rudder. I left Oklahoma without a clue as to my destination. I'd always done everything the hard way. Taking this into consideration, I decided to try something different, and ride out the rest of my stormy life in the "Big Easy." Everything I had amassed in my life had been whittled down to nearly nothing. I had my dog, a guitar, and a worn-out old Toyota camper.

In New Orleans, I managed to scrape out a meager living playing guitar in the French Quarter. When I was old enough to draw my Social Security, I did. Then I sold the camper and rented an apartment. I had lived without electricity or indoor plumbing for so long that such conveniences seemed almost unnatural. But as you can imagine, I acclimated rather quickly. Having a refrigerator was nice. Once again, I could keep mayonnaise, and of course, cold beer.

Having an apartment, and knowing that rent would never again be late, was most comforting. Before too long, Walmart, Good Will, and a considerable amount of dumpster diving, found the apartment fairly well furnished.

After almost a year living parked alongside one road then the next, and sleeping with one eye open for the cops, and the other eye open for thugs and gangsters, I didn't have much time for creature comforts. Once my retirement checks started coming... and I had a mailing address, I was once again a part of something, even if that something was just... the human race.

CHAPTER
TWO

I've worn long hair ever since I left home. My mother told me to get a haircut or move out! So, I did... Move out that is. I went lollygagging across the country hitch hiking with my guitar, and hopping freight trains. That was back in my Hippie days. I hit puberty slap dab in the big middle of the "Free love" movement.

The way I saw things back then was pretty simple. The way I figured it was this. If a man could play guitar and sing good enough to keep a little jingle in his pocket. If he could catch some leg in every other town he passed through, then why worry about the small stuff? Back then, girls and music were the only two things that made life worth living. That... and a little pot to smoke.

Those days are far behind me now. So far, in fact, they seem like two lifetimes ago. I still play and sing. I can still make a little "Hat money" with my guitar. Before I met Morilla, pussy and the affections of a woman, had pretty much become "pay as you go." The whores in New Orleans are pretty... Cheap too! Why a man can go pert near all the way around the world on a 20-dollar bill?

When supply outweighs demand, prices plummet! It's like playing Country music in Nashville, or the Blues in Memphis. You can't throw a rock in New Orleans without hitting either a musician or a whore! By the time I was 64, it wasn't uncommon at all for my living room to be piled up with either, or both.

Morilla Kaye Montgomery put a stop to all that, even though she didn't know it at the time. And then, it was a good spell more before I told her. By the time I did, we'd set up housekeeping together. I ran' em all off for a while there, but then I let the musicians back in, just not the whores.

I had a nice little 24-track recording studio in the apartment by that time. Nothing fancy, but all a man needs to lay down some righteous tracks, burn them to CD, and sell them puppies on Royal Street for Ten bucks a pop!

I was buying the blanks, engineering the sessions, and mastering the tracks. I'd hand the artist 10 CDs. He'd hand me 30 Bucks up front... No Credit... Period! When he sold out of CDs, I'd burn 10 more for him. Then he'd be back on Royal Street. Singing his heart out, playing his ass off, and hawking them CD's for all he was worth!

I worked sessions night and day for about six months. That was after I'd run the whores off. Well, all but one... I was recording whole bands and single artists. Pop, Jazz, Rock, and Country. Techno, Hip Hop, Grunge, Punk, Funk. Disco, Zydeco. It didn't make a shit to me. I was willing to record a mouse fart, as long as there was cash flow in it. All I wanted was to put back some money. I was gonna buy a ring for Miss Morilla Kaye Montgomery. Then I was gonna ask her on bended knee if she'd have me.

After I'd had more than 40 bands through the studio, I was looking at some pretty good side money... just by replenishing their product. I had two or three hundred a week coming in. It would have been more than that, but some of my artists were slick dicks. They'd have their girl-friends rip and burn copies just so they could put my cut in their own pockets. This was seldom the case with full bands. It was always the Guru anal types who were down to the last man, a pain in the ass to work with in the studio anyway.

Morilla Kaye and I had an internet romance. I'd heard of people falling in love online before, but I didn't take no stock in it. That is, not until it happened to me! We would drink coffee every morning back then. We would share pictures of our families, and our animals. She had two dogs, small ones like my dog Jazzy. Their names were Nigel and Sookie. We were then, and are to this day, big-time animal lovers.

We would drink coffee and shoot texts back and forth every morning. Looking back on it now, I'm most certain that was when the love bug began to fairly eat us both alive. When I heard my coffee pot gurgle, and my phone ding. When I looked and saw her messenger profile picture... why you couldn't have wiped the smile off my face with anything less than an ax handle?

I knew that all my years of struggle and failure had turned me into a drunk, but I couldn't tell her that. I was afraid she might leave me. I struggled with it for a month or so. Granny always said. "The truth is gonna' stand when the world burns down!" So... I just came on out with it. I told her neither I nor my dog had much of a pedigree. That my dog was a mutt, and I was a drunk. That all in all, I was a near-do-well and a misfit!

I told her about my sorry life. How it had been like a game of chess. That I'd been checked, and that I had been mated. How I had met a mess of women in this lifetime's run that I could live with... and how I had some of them. "But confound it I confessed... here I am... says I... 64 years old I told her. And then I say... There you are... Just now come along... the only darn woman on the planet that I can't live without!" I pushed (Send.) A second later the screen flashed... (Delivered.) "Well Says I... turning to my dog. "Guess that's that!"

CHAPTER
THREE

Turns out, the best thing I ever did for myself was to fess up. She met me with her heart most in the air. Like an Angel sent from Heaven, it was! In all my days, I'd never seen anyone with so much compassion. Her love fell on me like a Kangaroo steak on an Ozzie's Bar-B-Que pit! I was three whole days sober before I even knew what hit me!

When you're touched by an Angel, you begin to believe in miracles. I made up my mind right then and there! I was fixin' to straighten up and fly right... I was gonna' turn over a new leaf, just like Mama always said I should. I was gonna work myself over. I was gonna' spit and shine my ole ragged-edged self, til I was fittin' to be her suitor! I was gonna' take Morilla walking in the rain, just so I could throw my coat in a mud puddle, then grab her up, and carry her across the puddle anyway. I had made up my mind. I was gonna' do whatever it took, to win the hand of Morilla Kaye Montgomery.

From that day forward to this, my only necessity is to provide Morilla's daily dose of hugs and kisses. It took me a while to figure it all out. I'm not very smart when it comes to feelings and such. But Morilla is. She teaches me more and more about it all the time. What she's learned me so far, would fill a book if I were a'mind to pencil it all down. But I don't. Why should I? One word sums it all up. Puts it in a nutshell for me so to speak. Purpose... Morilla gives me purpose!

Now you take ole Mel Tillis for instance. Now that feller there? He's one of my favorites! Try and get him to talk without stuttering... He can't do it. Put a guitar in his hand, and strike up the band, and he'll never miss a lick... You wanna know why? I'll tell ya' why. When he sings, he has a purpose. That's just the same way I love Morilla.

CHAPTER

FOUR

My Morilla is most a Hoot on the riding mower. I'm glad we live far off the beaten path. If we lived in town, she might deny herself this most simple pleasure. When she pulls the lever that sets the blades to whirling? When the machine shakes, and groans under the strain? You can see her jaw set firmly in the transfer of power. Morilla morphs from the "be all... end all!" New York Times Best Selling Author, into a romping stomping 18 horse powered twin cylinder Wisconsin.

She mows down all opposition, just as she did as an activist in the Woman's Rights movement. She bounces along with her white-knuckled grip at 10 and 2, with that unmistakable Carol King look on her face. "I am Woman...hear me roar!

Even though my Morilla is somewhat of a celebrity in

literary circles, especially in the "Murder Mystery Category." Even though lawn maintenance is far beneath her pay grade. It is the only opportunity she has, to dawn her faded sun bonnet. The one that has been passed down to her by Morilla's great-grandmother. She loves it dearly... but would not be caught dead in it fashionably speaking.

I think the Satin Blue laced bow she's always tied strategically under her chin; may well be the very reason my weed eater starts every time! Many are the kisses I have stolen from beneath that Bonnet. It has preserved the freshness of her skin, and the sweet nectar of her lips since she was just a girl.

There isn't all that much grass to cut. It's just enough to get Morilla out from behind the computer every 10 days or so. She no sooner finishes one book than she's started on another. Where that woman gets her imagination is beyond me! I'll bet when she was a little girl, she could spin some whoppers!

Why that woman can come up with ways to kill a feller in their books, like ain't nobody ever heard tell of. I remember her killin' one ole boy so slick, he wasn't even dead till the mortician bled him out. The coroner said that the mortician was the one who really killed him.

Morilla had it all set up so, that the killer got off Scott free. Everyone who read that book knew it wasn't the mortician! Guess that's why them book worms took such a shine to it. That's the one that put her on top of the heap!

"When Dead Men Talk." That's what she called it. They had her on the TV... And the radio too!

I remember, her agent flew all the way down from New York City in a twin-engine Cessna. He said to pack up a few things, and come on... so, we did. I'd walked around a few airplanes in my time. I'd studied 'em out once in the Doctor's office going through the magazine rack. I never dreamed there was a man alive who could get me on one! Guess I never figured on Morilla though!

CHAPTER
FIVE

First thing ya' know we were stretched out across the sky, dancin' with the clouds, headed out for New York City. As soon as we hit the runway, a string of limousines came up alongside us. No sooner had we got stopped, but a big Black lady was tugging at Morilla. "Come on Honey... We're going shopping!

"Well, Joe." He says to me. His name is Joe too. Joe Bartello. He's Morilla's agent. I don't think he likes me much. "You'll get used to this before too long," he says, holding his chin and scrubbing his stubbly Italian whiskers like he seriously doubted that I'd stay in Morilla's life very much long enough that it would matter much anyway. "I suppose you better reckon I will." I retorted briskly as I leashed up the dogs.

My Limo driver stands resolutely at Parade rest. "Mr. Pie?" He addresses me hesitantly as if there was any possible way he could mispronounce my name. "That's me," I say. He tries to hide a snicker... but can't. "You can just call me Joe if that's easier for you though." He steps to the middle door of the Limo, puts one hand behind his back, and says. "Please mind to watch your head, Mr. Pie.

Before you know it, there we were. Slap dab in the middle of New York City. I push the button and roll down the window. I'd never been to New York City before that first trip. I didn't care much about being there anyway, but since I already was, I wanted to see it.

The window glass of the limo is always so dark, it looks like it must be midnight outside, but I know it couldn't be but half past five at the most. Nigel... he's first to the window. Sookie and Jazz are a photo finish for second place. All three of them have their heads hanging out, streaking the shiny Black limo with Doggie slobber. The driver... he looks most annoyed.

I holler at the driver. "Stop!" He doesn't hear me. Then I see the intercom button and I push it. "Stop!" I say again. He slides back the soundproof window looking more aggravated now than ever. "Yes Mr. Pie?" "Yea man," I say. Stop for a minute, my dogs need to pee!" He lets out a long-disgusted breath, leaving just enough wind in his pipes to reply... "As you wish, Mr. Pie."

Another mile of mostly city busses and taxi cabs roll by, then we turn into Central Park where we meander past acres of sprawling trees. About that time, Nigel sees a squirrel and makes a Tarzan leap out the window. He tares across the manicured grass and gives that ole grey squirrel a run for his money. Nigel ain't never caught a squirrel far as I know, but he catches this one! I'm fighting with the door handle trying to get out. I bust a Dukes of Hazard move and run slap dab over the Limo driver. Jazzy and Sookie come flying out the window right behind me. All three of us head for the tree where that squirrel and Nigel are having it... the fur was a-flyin'! When the squirrel saw the two more dogs coming, he gave ole Nigel a piece of his tail and skedaddled right on up that tree.

I was laughing so hard by that time that I didn't hear the Limo drive off. Nigel was whimpering on the count of his nose, but he wouldn't let loose of that squirrel's tail. His nose was torn up purdy good, but he was all right. I gathered all three leashes and headed back to where the Limo was, only to find that it was gone! That sap sucker had done drove off and left us. There was Morilla's suitcase, and my backpack, tossed in the grass by the road.

I brushed off my britches legs, snugged down my Stetson, strapped on the backpack, and picked up Morilla's suitcase. Then me and the kids struck out on foot. We hadn't walked more than a few blocks when I saw what I was looking for. There it was, tucked in among some buildings so tall that the clouds shadowed out the tops of 'em. Ritz Carlton: Central Park.

Even though I had a fresh coat of polish on my boots, and Morilla had pressed my Wranglers, I felt like a fish out of water around all those fancy folks. I straightened my collar and cinched up my Mississippi string tie, then walked right on in.

First thing off, was this big white Poodle dog with a puff on his tail big as a tennis ball. He wanted Nigel's squirrel tail. Nigel went to growling so deep the little feller vibrated. He didn't bark though. He couldn't bark with that tail in his mouth. Nigel was still in a fightin' mood! That fat lady's Poodle figured out purdy quick, he wasn't gonna get Nigel's squirrel tail, and that he'd better be watchin' out for his own! The fat lady, she snubbed us. She pulled on the leash of that Poodle dog and said. "Come along, Fredrick!"

The lady at the front desk was as nice as she could be. I told her who I was, and who Morilla was, and that our last name was Pie. She couldn't find our reservation at first, then I told her about Morilla, and how she uses her last name instead of mine because of her books and all. Morilla Kaye Montgomery? The lady inquired enthusiastically. "That's it!" says I... "THE" ... Morilla Kaye Montgomery? "When Dead Men Talk?" "That's her!" Says I... beaming with pride. "Do you think she'll sign my book?" She asks while producing a paperback copy from beneath the counter. "Wy, I know she will, Honey... she's sweet as pie!" The clerk and I both catch it at the same time, then we look at one another and bust out laughing and say simultaneously. "She is a Pie!"

CHAPTER
SIX

By that time in my life, I had stayed in my fair share of motels. It had always been a point of curiosity for me just what the difference was between a motel and a hotel. The Ritz Carlton showed me just as plain as the nose on your face. The best way I can say it is this: A motel is like a moth, and a hotel, is like a butterfly.

After we'd had our laugh, the lady behind the counter and me, she sprang into action. Before you could say "Jack Sprat," a slender old Black gentleman in a Red vest and a Captain's hat, had loaded up Morilla's suit case and my back pack on a wheeled cart and was leading us toward the elevators.

The kids walked in their usual formation. Nigel was out front, with Sookie half a stride behind and to the left, while Jazzy limped along to the right of Sookie.

The elevator ride to the 33rd floor seamed to last forever. I made small talk to the captain who responded with grunts and single words mostly. I rambled on and on, trying to drown out the sound of straining elevator cables, and one pulley in particular, that sounded like it could use a few pumps of grease.

Finally, the bell dinged, and we stepped out on the plush red carpet of the 33rd floor. The top floor of the famed Ritz Carlton: Central Park. The 33rd floor of the Ritz had been the topic of conversation only a few weeks ago on late-night radio. That night's program was about movie stars. Dead ones! Celebrities who had become so comfortable here at the Ritz, that they always come back, even after they were dead!

Ole George Noory interviewed a feller who went on and on about it. He used to be a Bell Boy here at the Ritz. Then he quit, just so he could write a book about it... He told me about Betty Grable and Greta Garbo. Liz Taylor, and how she always ran around in Baby Doll pajamas. Why to hear him tell it, she never wore nothin' but high heel shoes, and Baby Doll pajamas!

He talked about ole Hugh Hefner, and how his wheelchair left tracks in the carpet, but that only happened when the moon was full. Why that feller went on so, that a body would think he was bosom buddies with purt near everybody, who was anybody... when it comes to famous folks. He swore up and down that he saw 'em most every night.

Like there weren't nothin' to it. Even though they... and their lovers too... were deceased!

"Right dis' way Mer Pie," the captain said as we stepped off the elevator. He led us through a lavish Gallery, then down a cavernous hallway that ran along the far wall past a dazzling water feature whose colored beams of light bounced off the Chrystal-laden chandeliers. The Chrystal sent splinters of light bouncing gleefully like a Broadway show off the vast rotunda sealing. Some shards of light were caught up in the politics of dancing. Some were voted down and bounced out turning the elegant Crystals every color in the rainbow. Why you ain't never seen sich a sight!

The hallway leading to room 333, fairly came alive with the wonderfully simple, but profound work of Norman Rockwell. His paintings seemed to jump from the walls in celebration. Splashing my eyes with colors so rich they just seemed to pop! It was as if their pallet had been reserved for those whose life path would find them on the 33rd floor of the Ritz Carlton. Central Park...Right in the very heart of New York City!

The dogs made themselves at home right away. Nigel hiked his leg on an umbrella holder just inside the door. Then he strategically placed his squirrel tale between the holder and the wall. He laid down with his tattered nose right next to the hard-won squirrel's tale, like he was guarding the Arc of the Covenant.

I tipped the ole Captain ten bucks after he unloaded

Morilla's suitcase and my backpack on the floor of our luxurious hotel suite. Ten bucks seemed more than plenty to me! The ole Captain looked at that ten-dollar bill like it was Monopoly money, but he took it just the same... I watched him pushing his cart back down the hallway shaking his head from side to side, and mumbling something about "Tight ass nigga's."

Sookie jumped up on the bed and dug herself out a pillow. Jazzy followed me as I checked out the lavish marble bathroom. There were mirrors everywhere! It had a big oval tub and a shower with six sprayer heads. There was a hose with a sprayer head on the end of it. It looked like something you might rinse dishes with, but I was most certain it wasn't, it was much too fancy for that. "Maybe feminine hygiene I reckoned. Then I looked around at Jazzy. That's when it hit me... A dog wash... That's what it is... a dog wash! "Well now... Doesn't that beat it all? Look Jaz... a dog wash!"

After flying in the Cessna and getting dumped in Central Park. After navigating the rude stares of all those fancy folks and that fat lady and her poodle dog. I was glad to be settled. I couldn't wait to see Morilla. As excitable as she was, I knew she would be bursting at the seams with a flurry of bubbles.

I also knew I'd be seeing the ole Captain again. His cart would be loaded down with hat boxes and fur coats and no telling what all. That big Black lady that snatched Morilla?

You can bet your bottom dollar she knows all about fashion and all the latest styles... and how to spend Joe Bartello's money! I'll give the ole Captain another Ten spot... but this time by golly... He'll earn his money!

I fiddled around with the TV for a while. I thumbed through most a million channels but couldn't find Gun Smoke or the Cartwright's or a single Western one, so I slung my ole Stetson at the bed post. It landed on the Brass knob and spun like a horseshoe. "Ringer" ... I shouted in a tone of victory. Then I slipped off my cowboy boots and lay down on the bed. I was trying hard to wait up for Morilla, but she'd wake me up I reckoned. Besides...I was plum tuckered out.

Sookie greeted me with a lick across the kisser. She and I became thick as thieves right from the start. Nigel had taken a little longer though. He is very protective of Morilla. At first, he was not too eager to share her affections with me. This too would pass as he found himself enthralled with Jazzy's affections the first time she came in season.

Looking back now, it's kind of' funny how it all happened. Things were starting to get edgy between Morilla and me. We were desperately in love with one another. Neither of us wanted to cheat just because we needed touch. All the lovin' we got was over our computers or the telephone line. As time went by, we found a way to find some relief though. We'd lay up in the bed naked as the day we were born. Her up in Texas, and me down in New Orleans. We'd talk about how good it was gonna' be when we finally got to hold one another. Then, the first thing you know, her voice would come across the telephone smooth as freshly churned butter. She'd carry on so, that I could almost taste her lips. Morilla cooed words in my ear that was like dipping your finger in the honey jar.

Me... I'd drop down low... like Barry White. Then I'd sing grainy, and deep. It didn't seem to bother Morilla much that the only words I knew were... "Darlin' I... I can't get enough of your love Baby!" I'd sing the same words over and over. Before too long, her breath would get shallow, and fast. Me... Long about that time, I'd let out a low moan howl like a lovesick bull moose. Afterwords, she'd seem all shy and timid like. Me, I'd talk her up soft. Then she'd be happy, and plum full of bubbles all over again.

CHAPTER

SEVEN

Love between us began to bloom with the flowers of Spring that year. We'd actually met in person several times some years earlier. I had the Pizza joint in Medicine Park Oklahoma back then. Medicine Park was Morilla's hometown. Her mother still lived in the park. When she came to visit, she'd always stop by for pizza. Even though she kept popping up in my life, I never had the first clue that she was attracted to me. I've always been one of those people who love with blinders on. I had Barbara in my focus back then.

One day after I had the apartment in New Orleans, Morilla posted a comment on my Face Book page. That's when we started chatting regularly. The seeds she tried to plant years ago had finally found fertile soil. All that held us apart now, were the miles between us. After I sold the Toyota camper, I no longer had transportation except for my Western Flyer.

I turned 65 years old that August. I awoke on my birthday and put on coffee. By then I was resigned to the fact that this was just going to be another day. Little did I know that prayers I was afraid to pray, were going to come true anyway.

Jazzy did her usual pee dance by the front door, stopping intermittently to check the progress I was making by tying my shoelaces. I poured a steaming cup as I asked the little Papillon the question she was always anxious to hear. "Who wants to go to the park?"

Jazz would always shake with uncontrollable excitement as I snapped on her leash. She would burst through the open door with her insatiable appetite for life. She was ready to reclaim her space. Cats that happened to be in the yard would stare at first, then they would scatter. She dragged me to the park that morning, eager as always to check her Pee mail.

My birthday fell on a Wednesday that year. Just another sign that this birthday would be insignificant. The stream of bicycle traffic on the hike and bike trail was at its usual ebb and flow. Rare is the occasion to see cyclists dressed in spandex. Few and far between are the Lance Armstrong types.

Bicycles are a typical mode of transportation here in

NOLA. Just as typical as a pickup truck is in Texas. Food service workers in skid-proof shoes; White starched shirts; Black pants and matching bow ties. Street musicians with guitars strapped to their backs. Art gallery women in hi-heel shoes, peddling their prissy asses to the French Quarter where they lock their bikes, then morph into elegant ladies of the arts.

Jazz and I walked our usual route that morning. Past the basketball court, then up and around the swimming pool. From the corner of my eye, I couldn't help but notice a slender blonde woman swaying gently on the swing set over by the Merry-Go-'Round. I was in awe of her loveliness. I led Jazzy off the hike and bike trail into a cluster of trees. From the shade of an Oak, I watched as she gave her little dogs a ride on the swing. She held them in her lap one at a time.

As we watched, Jazzy's ears perked. Her tail began to wag so hard it looked like she was dancing. With a sudden burst of enthusiasm, she hit the end of her leash and fairly flew... like she'd been shot from a cannon! Just about the time I realized the Blonde headed lady was Morilla, Morilla realized it was Jazzy running to her.

"Jazzy... Jazzy... Is that you?" Then she looked up and saw me coming. I'll never forget the way she shrieked with joy!

I walked toward the swings as the four of them frol-icked like long-lost friends. When our eyes met, I tried to contain myself, but it was no use. I welled up fairly bursting with joy and cried. It was really her in the flesh! Morilla Kay Montgomery!

As the dogs darted to and fro in an eager game of catch and sniff, Morilla and I embraced. We held one another ever so gently at first. Both of us were afraid of the disappointment that might be incurred if the object of our affections were in fact, just a figment of our own imaginations. Imaginations brought on by a need so deep, that reality had become stranger than fiction.

So much was on the line. She trembled like a baby bird in my hands as I held her more firmly. My own heart was still in shock as it pounded out an ancient rhythm that God had scored and orchestrated in the garden of Eden. It was not a beat of solidarity. It was a rhythm designed to be celebrated in unison. Our hearts matched so perfectly that it was as if they'd found their own tempo and began to dance in perfect harmony. Each beat is a complement to the last. The next beat was anticipated, as though our hearts were destined to dance through eternity.

In my arms it seemed... she had found her rightful place. A place she'd dreamed of long ago, and finally found. Her coffee-brown eyes shone through pleading fearful tears. Tears rolled down tender cheeks as if to say; "Please don't hurt me." I kissed them one by one, as they mixed with my own.

As we walked along the hike and bike trail holding

hands and laughing, our red swollen eyes caught the atten-tion of passers-by. All who saw us likely assumed that we'd had an awful fuss, and were overjoyed to be back in the tinder arms of love. Nigel and Sookie followed Jazzy as she proudly led her new family back to the apartment.

CHAPTER

EIGHT

Morilla fell in love with New Orleans. When September came, we piled up and went to Round Rock Texas to check on her house. It was nice and roomy. A brick home setting on two lots. Her home was paid for, she was debt-free. Morilla had always been steady. She worked from her teenage years all the way up to full retirement. She retired from an accounting firm in Austin. We hung out a couple of days... I mowed the lawn, then we headed back to NOLA and my one-bedroom apartment.

The rest of that Summer flowed like warm Maple syrup over a hot stack of buttery pancakes. I was surprised to find how savvy Morilla was when it came to making money. The first thing she did was rent the upstairs apartment above mine. Between the two of us, we had both places.

Morilla was methodical in the way she went about

renting her apartment. She had a plan from the beginning. She pulled it off too! I remember just how she did it. After we got back from Round Rock she put her plan into action.

The first thing she wanted to do was to throw a BBQ in the courtyard. "Be sure to invite the "Landlord," she told me. "Oh... he'll be here whether you invite him or not. Ole James, he loves a party." "Good!" She said with distinct intention in her voice.

I dropped the word to a few musician friends. Free food and booze is all it took. The Bar-B-Q was on for that next Saturday afternoon. John B. and Angel showed up. So did Dingus the fiddle player and Stagger lee. Stag was a young gunslinger out of Carolina. He brought his Telecaster and a pretty little minx who'd picked him up at a gig the night before. In no time at all, the courtyard was plum full of folks, including James the landlord.

Right away it became obvious to me that Morilla was penning the needle on her... "Charm-O-Meter." "James," Morilla says as she pours a fresh glass of wine for them both. "I'd sign a six-month lease on that upstairs apart- ment." James looks at Morilla and says; "It's monfh to monfh Missy! Never you mind about no lease... All I axe is dat ya' pay da' rent proper, like ole Joe dare." Ain't no need for all dat paperwork Morilla. Sep for da rent receipt. Dat's only one a momfh." The land lord added.

Morilla smiled as she wrapped her long slender fingers around a swirling glass of Sherry. Her Almond shaped eyes grew even larger as her chin jutted upward along with her wine glass. Honey Gold's hair danced with the twist of her shoulders as she struck a pose of obvious contemplation.

"I only do business in a business-like fashion, James. I need a six-month lease for my own protection. I'll pay to have the lease drawn up. After all, it is for my own protection." She said in a timid voice "However you want to dooz it Miss Morilla." "Then we have a deal, Mr. Taylor?" Morilla offered her hand. James could not deny himself the chance to touch her hand and take the money for her first month's rent. His eyes told me that he had felt both the softness and the firmness in her handshake as they sealed the bargain. I didn't know just how, but somehow, I knew... Ole James? He'd just been had!

In the years that followed, I watched her tame some of the biggest cats in the publishing industry. One way or another... Morilla always got her way.

The lease her lawyer drew up was bullet proof. Airtight! It gave Morilla every right to Sub-Lease the upstairs apartment as an Air B&B. After the lease was signed. Once the (I's) were dotted and the (T's) were crossed, she got on her laptop and ordered a mess of stuff from Amazon.

Together, she and I slapped on a fresh coat of paint in the upstairs apartment.

The paint barely had time to dry before a caravan of delivery trucks started showing up. They delivered sheets, pillowcases, and curtains. Pots and pans and plates with matching saucers. Bedroom furniture and a new living room suit. Everything anyone could possibly need to set up housekeeping came in on the trucks.

After the new curtains were hung and the bed was made. When the cupboard was slam full of new dishes and coffee cups. While we were hanging a great big mirror behind the new sofa, I said to her. "Morilla," says I... "I'm sure gonna' miss you!" "What do you mean Joe?" "Well," says I. "With your new fancy apartment and all, I prolly won't be seeing near so much of you." Morilla laughed hardily. Then she took me by the hand and led me back to her new bedroom and loved me up good.

In a sudden spell of weakness, I let my insecurity show. "I don't know how many fellers are gonna' tumble here on your new mattress Honey," says I. "But at least I was the first!" Morilla burst out laughing. Then she came up off her pillow and started licking me like a cat-lapping buttermilk. She made swirls with her tongue, starting at my belly button and working her way down. It was the first time she'd ever kissed me down there. She'd say a few sultry words, then go right back to lickin'. I liked it better when she didn't talk, because what she said when she did talk, fairly broke my heart in two!

Her voice was rich with mystery. There was a tone to it that made me arch and stand like a flag pole. When she did come up for air, she talked about all the men who were gonna get lucky right there on that mattress. Big men, short men, tall men, fat men. She said there were sure to be some Black men too. That's alright she added, as long as they've paid in full first.

This fretted me so, that I lost my boner. She laughed out loud and pointed with her finger at ole Porky. He was leaning like the tower of Pizza. Then he fell so hard ole Porky bumped his head! Morilla realized then that she'd had her fun. Even though she hadn't lied. It was time for her to tell the whole truth. What she'd been planning all along. "It's an Air B & B Joe... a short-term rental for the tourists. Our first guests will be here on the fifth of September. $250.00 a night... and we're already booked up until the 16th of October. We can get twice that for Halloween. Then the prices go up all the way up through Mardi Gras!

"How did you get Blonde hair, and brains at the same time, Honey?" I asked her. After her truth set in on me and my insecurity was gone. I came to terms with the fact that she had unknowingly made a fool of me. I maintained my compassion, but still, I knew it was my turn now. I pulled her back into my arms and gently pushed her ankles up around her ears. I kissed her deeply, then drove ole Porky to the hilt! Yes indeed... Porky was in retaliation mode!

CHAPTER

NINE

The short-term rental brought in money hand over fist. Morilla was raking in Hundred Dollar Bills, like a yard man rakes leaves in the Fall. James, the landlord was mad as hell! He tried to cause trouble, but Morilla's attorney sewed him. When they delivered his court summons, He quit hassling us about the money she was making with her savvy business sense... and his modest apartment.

My life before Morilla had been a never-ending procession of rough and rocky roads. I was always either hitting the gas... Or pumping the brakes. Before I knew it, Morilla had me on cruise control. For the very first time in my life, I had finally found a rhythm. Love with her was like a dance... And boy were we in the pocket!

It wasn't any time at all until I became a spoiled rascal.

Why you've never seen sich as the like! Morilla ordered my clothes online. She did that every Tuesday for the first little while. Come the following Monday, I'd have a whole week's worth of new clothes. She'd lay 'em out on the bed for me every morning. She was trying to teach me what went with what. Morilla knew everything there was to know about fashion. She could dress a Philadelphia lawyer or a crusty ole singin' cowboy like myself.

Now Morilla, she was sure right about that new mattress in the upstairs apartment. Why there'd be a new couple up there most every night, trying to knock the stuffings outta' that new Posturepedic. Me and Morilla, we'd broken it in purdy good. Well, for a couple of older folks. Sometimes, it would sound like a full-fledged rodeo going on upstairs!

The Air b&b was laid out just like our downstairs apartment. So, the upstairs bedroom was just above our downstairs bedroom. Sometimes when our upstairs guest got too carried away on that new Posture-pedic, Morilla would crawl outta' bed, and go to cleaning house. But sometimes she would put on her fish net stockings and her stilettos, snug down her Stetson and ride me so hard, it was all I could do to make eight seconds! She'd throw back her head, dig in her heels, and fairly jump me outta' the chute!

CHAPTER

TEN

We ran the streets a lot back in those days. We'd set up our music show at the "Red Door." Or in front of "The Brick Wall." Or on the corner of Royal Street and Dumaine, which was Morilla's favorite place to play. I can't recall us ever having more fun than we did in those days!

Back then, I'd strum a few licks on my guitar just to set up a rhythm. Then Morilla would go to slappin' the tambourine or popping her spoons. I'd let out a low moan holler like I was full gospel and was fixin' to be struck down by the Holy Ghost. Then I'd go to singin' my ole country heart out. Afore ya' know it, we'd be stirrin' up such a commotion, we'd be stoppin' em touristas in their tracks. They'd go to throwing money like it was catchin' their pants afire! Morilla, she'd be dancin', and workin' up such a rhythm that any foot, what was a foot, couldn't stop their toes from dancin'. Jazzy, she'd point her muzzle up toward Heaven, and let out a high mournful howl. That would get Sookie and Nigel goin' too! Yes indeed! There we were... The Five Pie Family Band breaking it all down in the very heart of New Orleans, slap dab in the middle of the French Quarter! Between our retirement checks and the music money, we were able to save every penny we made from the Air B&B.

For Morilla, our playful life was like a dream come true. She had been tied down to a highly stressful job most all her life. From an early age, she'd had all the responsibilities that come with being a certified public accountant, and a homeowner. Her new career as a Murder Mystery writer was starting to garner some favorable attention, but had by no means reached its full potential. She figured a regular change of scenery might broaden her horizons and increase her creativity.

As long as she had her laptop, she could write from anywhere. Retirement and technology had finally made travel an option for her. Throwing caution to the wind, we bought a motor home and began to tie up loose ends. The Five Pie Family Band was going on the road!

James changed his tune when Morilla's lease was up. Having recouped her original investment and yielding profits enough to pay cash for the motor home. Morilla turned the Air B&B lock stock and barrel over to James... along with a laptop dedicated to running the business. All the previous customers, along with current and future reservations. The business's Tax numbers, the liability insurance policy information, along with the agent's name. All she kept was the proceeds accumulated in the Air B&B account.

James's granddaughter moved into my apartment, the same day Morilla and I took off in the motor home. She was going to manage the Air B&B for her Papaw.

ELEVEN

Our first destination was Big Pine Key Florida. It was a good stretch and got us used to maneuvering the motor home through tole booths and McDonald's drive-thru lanes. Or not! The 28-footer was both too long and too tall to negotiate a drive-thru. For a while, we watched the overpasses on the scenic routes which we preferred. It seemed as if we'd just barely make it under them, but we always did.

Morilla wouldn't drive on the two-lane roads, or under stop lights. She was strictly an Interstate Highway girl. Morilla loved the truck drivers. She loved to flirt with them on the C.B. It wasn't long until she had their lingo down pat. The truckers loved her too!

"Breaker one nine. How 'bout that Psycho Beaver? Got your ears on?" "That's a big ten four. You got the Psycho

Beaver; come on" ... "Hey good lookin'... Whatcha' got cookin'?" This seemed to be a typical scenario for the antics that would play out just as soon as Morilla got behind the wheel. Morilla had christened our motor home, "The Gypsy Traveler."

Morilla would blow as many kisses as it took to land us in the, "Smokey-free-zone." Better known as "The rocking chair." Boy could that girl make some time! Both on the highway... and with the truckers!

Big Pine Key was a journey through the past for me. I had lived on Big Pine as an 18-year-old pot-smoking Hippie, wet behind the ears and fresh out of high school. By day, I worked for D.R. Gaines construction company. My job was to grade a thin layer of gravel on the bottom of the ditch before the Hydra-Crane swung a 20-foot section of cast iron pipe over the ditch and then lowered it down to be slid into the rubber gasket of the previously laid pipe. By night, I would drink beer and smoke pot with all my Big Pine buddies.

The party would start directly after work. The crew would pile up and go to Ogie Malone's store, and throw back a few cold ones underneath the Sapodilla tree. We'd smoke so much pot that a body would swear we were trying to burn a hole in the ozone. When we were all comfortably numb, we'd head out to the bar, or to Pearl Trailer Park where we'd join in the campfire circle that usually started when the moon came up, and the girls came out.

No one had been raised in the Florida Keys. There were no parents or grandparents within a hundred miles. Accountability was a lifestyle the establishment had invented. It was their prison; not ours. We were free to live unencumbered by their rules and expectations. Sex had no ties to long-term commitment. It was simply a matter of physical attraction. Nothing less would do. Nothing more was expected. It was what the news media called, "The Free Love" movement.

I took the wheel on the outskirts of Miami and roaded the Gypsy Traveler south on the narrow two-lane roads and across a multitude of bridges that span the mangrove swamps and bay areas that leapfrog all the way to Key West. I'll never forget the look on Morilla's face when we motored through Marathon, and she saw the Seven Mile Bridge for the first time.

The Seven Mile Bridge stretches like a gray concrete ribbon whose destination must surely be the edge of the earth. The sun shone bright as a polished lemon in a perfect cloudless sky on that particular day. The bridge could be seen to the curvature of the earth, where it appeared to end, and just drop off the world. The bridge was two-way traffic, and the lanes were narrow. Morilla's eyes got as big as saucers when she realized just how narrow. "Whoever designed this bridge must have driven a Volkswagen!" Morilla declared.

When we got to the middle of the bridge where nothing but water could be seen in any direction, she crossed her arms and leaned back in the seat. Then she put one bare foot on the dashboard and looked at me as if I were owed an explanation. "I put one foot up because I don't want to pee down both legs," she said in the tone of a frightened child. This throttled me! I began to laugh uncontrollably. This was a crossing that I knew was safe because I had traversed the bridge literally hundreds of times back in the day. I was in complete control, even though I convulsed with laughter.

"Look, Honey! There she is... Big Pine Key! Morilla had ridden the whole way with her eyes closed and a sullen look on her face. It was good to see her smile again. She bounced her feet off the floorboard and pumped her arm victoriously.

After we cleared the seven-mile bridge, we made a right-hand turn onto the Key Deer Refuge. Morilla had requested a stop. "You need to pee?" I ask. "No... I already did." She said matter-of-factly. She showed only a tiny tinge of embarrassment as she spoke. "I just wanna' change these pissy pants. This brought on a round of laughter that she took part in this time.

There we were parked on the shoulder of Refuge Road, where it intersects U.S. Highway 1. We were at the very spot where our construction crew tied into that water main almost 50 years ago. The main traversed the Seven Mile Bridge from Marathon bringing fresh water to Big Pine Key, and points beyond.

The earth had long since healed from the wheel trencher that cut through the coral rock. The track-mounted trencher left a continuous conveyor belt spun pile of seashell-laden coral along the trench that lay open back then until the entire pipeline had been pressure tested and declared worthy. Only then could our miles of back-breaking work be covered with Bull Dozers and tamped down with pavement rollers.

Morilla wiped down her seat with paper towels and Windex while the kids walked with me down memory lane. They took a pee because they needed to. I took a pee just for old times' sake. I reveled in the simplicity of my life back then. How thick and long my hair was. How Bronze the Florida sun had made my skin while working eight hours a day in cutoff blue jeans, work boots, and a hard hat.

"Y'all about ready?" It was Morilla. I sprung forward from the trance that had held me spell bound in my flood of remembrances. "Sure Babe!" "Come on Nigel. Come on Sookie. Jazz, come on. Morilla clapped her hands. Come on y'all... load up! She caught me in a loving embrace: "I'm sorry I was such a bitch. That bridge just scared the piss outta' me!" She declared. "I'll say it did!" "Oh, you!"

She squealed as she caught her own funny.

"Oh, look I exclaimed... There's the old forestry tower!" "Did you ever get laid way up there Joe?" A look of guilt must have taken my face... "Don't lie." She teased. "Morilla, you know me all too well." "I don't want to know about it." She said pretending to be mad. "You'll just have to take me up there and show me!" "The forestry tower has a wood floor," I warned. Be sure and bring a pillow for your butt." I cautioned her. "Janie always forgot hers," I added teasingly. Morilla attacked me playfully. "You ass hole!"

The speed limit was 25 miles per hour. "Strictly Enforced." The signs said in a font and size that would make most drivers err on the side of caution. As I roaded the "Gypsy Traveler" cautiously down the road, Morilla began to read to me from her phone. "Big Pine Key was set aside by The United States National Wildlife Service in 1957 as a reserve for the preservation of "Key Deer." They were becoming endangered due to poaching and hot rod racing. Morilla read further noting that the deer are closely monitored by signal collars fitted by the Wildlife Fish and Game Commission.

"Who was the Governor of Florida in 1957?" I ask inquisitively. (Morilla loved to do research.) She rattled the keys on her phone and a few seconds later she stated the answer matter-of-factly... "LeRoy Collins. Now it's my turn to ask a question. "Where's the freshwater pond the alligator lived in?" "That's where I'm taking you now, Sweetheart." I retorted. I had told Morilla all about the freshwater pond, and how I used to play my harmonica before I bathed in it all those many years ago. I used to live in a box truck on the job sight in the early 70s when gasoline was in such short supply in the Keys.

I cut my wheels to the left and rolled up in the same spot I used to park my ole box truck back in the day. "This is it," I announced as another flood of memories came back to me. "I wonder if the ole alligator is still here?" I wondered out loud. "We better leave the kids inside until we find out Joe." "How long do you think alligators live?" She asks. Before I could tell her that I didn't have a clue, she was already Googling it. "About 50 years!" She exclaimed excitedly. "He could still be alive!" "There's only one safe way to find out." Says I. A question came across Morilla's face... "A harmonica?" she asks. "You got it, Babe!" I leaned over and pulled a 10-hole Marine Band Blues harp from the glove compartment. "Come on!" Says I.

Morilla and I sat on the bank as I slurried up a dredge of Blind Dog Fulton and some Smoke House Brown. I hadn't played but a few riffs, till here he came swishing his long tail across the pond. Morilla stood up as he got closer and closer. Then I stood up. "Is that him Joe?... Joe... Do you think that's him?" "Why 'coarse it is! Do you know any other alligators that like my harmonica playin'?" I ask jest fully.

The ole gator stopped short of coming on the bank. He

seemed to listen contently as I blew a few more passages with a mournful drone. I couldn't help but serenade my old friend. Morilla and I walked hand in hand to the further shore, and waded in the crystal-clear water, always remembering to keep a close eye on my old friend. It was amazing for me to share a piece of my childhood, with the woman who had come to be the love of my life.

After the thousand-mile journey from New Orleans to the Florida Keys, we were ready to chill for a few days and enjoy the amenities of our new motorhome. It was warm enough to swim in the ocean and explore the shops and restaurants. We were both eager to catch the local vibe.

Morilla was excited about starting the first book she was going to write on the road. She hadn't even landed on a title yet, but I could tell she was ready to kill the hell out of some poor pitiful bastard! I'd read a good bit of her work and the one think I found in common with all the unfortunate victims was this: If you gave them a choice on how they would meet their demise, the last choice they'd make would be the very way they'd bite the big one. On the upside for the poor unfortunates was this: Her imagination had so much trickery in it, that they'd be cold in the ground before they ever figured out how she killed them! I'll bet even the Devil considers her cunning deceitful ways most un-Godly!

CHAPTER
TWELVE

"Joe... hey Joe... Wake up, Joe!" "What is it, Honey?" "Some one's knocking at the door." "Okay... Okay, Baby! Just a minute." I slipped on my bath robe and made my way to the front of the coach. "Open up in there! Park patrol." I reached and got my billfold from off the console. Then I swung the door open.

"What's the trouble officer?" "No overnight camping! Can't you read the signs fella?" The little guy's hand shook as he held out his Wildlife and Fisheries badge. His Smokey the Bear hat looked like his Dumbo ears were all that was holding it up. It was plain that the little feller was either mad or scared. "Well now, says I. Don't you have to be able to read to get one of these?" I reached out and handed him my driver's license. "Louisiana Uh? I'll need to see your registration and proof of insurance too fella!"

I shouted back to Morilla. "Honey... I need coffee!" Then I addressed the Park Ranger. "Now officer," I say. "I'm a Park Ranger!" He interjects. "Well now then, Ranger. If you look at my driver's license where it says: Name? You can see that my name is not fella... It's Pie." "Yea, I saw that, he smirks. I figured with a name like Pie, you'd rather be called Fella." The little guy puts his hand over his mouth and tries to quell his laughter, but can't. He chuckles so hard, that his tan Khaki pants start to sag around his waste. He screws them back up, then tips his hat so he can see again.

"Sorry 'bout that Sir... It's just that... Pie... Well, that is kind of a funny name..."

Yea... So's Fife... You ever get tired of people calling you Barney? I say with a chuckle of my own. A blush takes his face... this time, I know he's mad!

Morilla reaches past me and hands Barney the registration and proof of insurance. "Here ya' go Officer," she says. I'm a Ranger! He reiterates, holding out his Badge for Morilla to see. "Why you sure are!" Morilla retorts like a grade schoolteacher to a fifth grader. "Okay... well then... you want some coffee, Ranger?" "No... He says while handing Morilla back the paperwork. "I just want you folks out of the Park!" With that, he turned and walked back toward his patrol car.

From a safe distance, Barney turned and looked back. With one hand on his hip, he reared his shoulders back and pointed a finger at me... "I've got my eye on you Pie!" When he did, I waved and said, "Say Hey to Goober for me! As he drove away, we both burst out laughing... "What a Schmuck!" Morilla howled.

The sun's glow was beginning to filter through the trees now. Barney had passed buy several times that night but didn't stop. The dew was heavy on the grass as we walked the dogs for their early morning duty call. I made a trip around the Gypsy Traveler inspecting tires and making sure the bicycles were strapped securely, and everything was in its place. Then with Barney as our escort, we headed back the way we'd come the previous afternoon. As we passed the forestry tower, Morilla leaned over and wrapped both her arms around my neck. "I still want us to do the forestry tower... Screw Barney!" She exclaimed.

We pull in to the parking lot where Ogie Malone's store used to be. The small wood-framed building has been replaced by a modern storefront. It's called: "Tote- A- Poke." The Sapodilla tree is gone. There is a tall cyclone fence with (NO SMOKING) signs attached to it. A Propane refilling station has taken the place of the pic-nick table where the crew used to drink beer after work. We grab a coffee and a bag of jelly doughnuts, then head south on highway one toward Key West.

At the southernmost point of the United States, we stand among scads of what Floridians call "Snowbirds." There's a telescope mounted on a stand that costs fifty cents. We drop in a couple of quarters in the slot to gaze at the churning ocean with its white-capped sprays of misty waves, and seabirds that are unaware of us.

Morilla insists that we take a few selfies for her social media page. Then we board The Gypsie Traveler and meander down the narrow streets of Key West. She is in search of the magic Hemingway seemed to find as his inspiration here on the island. That's when an inspiration of my own hits me. "Let's see if we can find the old Pearl Trailer Park." You think it's still there?" Morilla asks in a doubtful tone. "I doubt it, but let's look anyway.

All I remember of Pearl Trailer Park was a bunch of dilapidated old trailers no one in their right mind would live in... Except for a bunch of pot-smoking peace sign-waving, free-loving flower children. Those days were gone forever. What we did find surprised us both. Things had changed so much, I'd had a hard time finding it, but finally did. Everything about the park had changed, including the sign. Pearl-RV-Park. That's how the sign reads now.

Morilla reached over and took my hand. "Wanna' try it?" She asks. "We have to sleep somewhere tonight. I'm tired of Wal Mart parking lots... And I had all I wanted of Barney last night and this morning... "Sure Honey... we're already here... and I'm tired of driving.

Morilla read from the Owner's Manual and instructed me point by point as I hooked up the septic system. The hardest part of that job was finding the septic hose. It was stashed in the square tubing bumper. "Now ain't that handy as a pocket on a shirt, I exclaimed when Morilla finally found it in the Owner's Manual. Then right there under the dash, we found the automatic leveling button. One push of the button and the Gypsy Traveler felt like she was perched on the rock of Gibraltar, and level as a duckbill flattop.

I was messing with the roll out awning. It was giving me fits. I'd get one side down. Then when I pulled the other side down, the first side would start rolling back up. The awning was White with Blue stripes and had a ruffle across the front. "It's nice enough looking, I said under my breath. Now if only I could get the dad burn thing to stay put.

"Looks like you could use a hand their neighbor." I turned to see the person who was addressing me in such a friendly manner. He was wearing a light blue shirt with a White jacket, and pants to match. There was a gaudy chunk of Gold hanging from his neck on a Gold rope chain Mr. Tee would have been proud of.

The chunk was in the shape of a fiddle, like the one in Charlie Daniel's song. If it wasn't for the Rainbow-colored suspenders that held his pants up, he would have looked plum elegant! He was short, but a big man with snow White hair and a beard. My name's Simmons, Buck Simmons." He said stepping forward. "Pleased to meet ya' Buck. My name's Pie, Joe Pie. A smile took his face, but he never laughed. Lots of folks laugh at my name, but Buck didn't. I liked him right off.

Buck was one of those guys who could tell you how to do something, without being bossy about it. (The first sign of a good leader.) He kinda' like makes it look like the whole thing was your idea. "Now what if you get that side Joe, and I'll get this side? Then we'll pull down together? Does that sound like it might work Joe?" "Let's give it a try Buck. I say.

We pulled together and sure enough, the awning rolled out just like it ought to. "Now... said Buck. The way mine works, is you fasten these brace rods to the main frame of the awning pole." He takes him and slips it right in place. Me. I struggle. "It's too short," I say. "Loosen up that (T) bolt there in the middle of the brace rod and see if it will extend some maybe." I did what he said to do... and of course, it worked.

Buck and I stood off admiring our handy work. "That's a nice rig! Buck said admiringly, hands on his hips. "Thanks Buck... She drives and rides just like she ought to." I replied, even more convinced now than I already was.

"Want some Sweet Tea?" Came a voice from behind us. The offer came from Buck's wife. "Don't mind If I do. Thank ya' Mam." Says I. "Joe, this here's my wife Sadie." Please to meet ya' Mam!" "Sadie. This here's our new neighbor Joe." "And this here's Morilla y'all" ... I say as she comes walking up. Morilla, this here's Buck and Sadie.

Another introduction goes all 'round, "including the dogs." Another glass of Sweet Tea for Morilla, and we were all set. The girls went next door to Buck and Sadie's while I gave Buck the grand tour of The Gypsy Traveler. Buck noticed my guitar right off. "You a Picker?" He asked. "I bang around some," I say. "I got an ole fiddle I like to rosin up the bow on ever once in a while." Says Buck. "You look like a fiddler!" Says I. "Well... says Buck. He leans over and puts his hand on my shoulder. "That's how I got Sadie... and that's good enough for me."

THIRTEEN

"Y'all want some more Sweet Tea?" It was Sadie. She caught us just as we were coming back outside. Morilla was right there beside her. "Joe, you've gotta' see there rig. It's an Air Stream! And just as nice as it can be!" "Well now... why don't y'all come around for dinner?" Suggested Buck. I'll show her to ya' Joe." "Sadie already invited us. Spouts Morilla excitedly... and I already said yes!" "Well, I guess that just about settles it then," I say as Morilla snuggles her arm around my waist.

"Sadie, Ole Joe here is a guitar picker," Buck says. "You don't say!" Sadie exclaims joyfully. She turns to Morilla; Buck's been looking for a guitar picker, he played the last one to death!" She clapped her hands together and reared her head back in laughter. "Morilla... Buck plays fiddle." Says I. "Oh, Lord!" Exclaims Morilla turning to Sadie.

"They'll be starting up a band before you know it!" Bucks already got one... He plays everywhere we go."

"You'll meet the boys. There are three more Air Streams full of 'em! We're all retired Dentists." He adds. "Yea, interjects Sadie, and every last one of them has false teeth!" We all rolled with laughter. This Sadie gal. She and Morilla are already like two peas in a pod! "Well, folks... Just about dark is when we usually set down to eat. Is that alright with y'all? Sounds good to me. Morilla nods approvingly.

The Simmons collected their tea glasses. "See y'all then," I say as they head back across the patch of grass between our patio and theirs.

I walked around to the back of the R.V. and unstrapped our bicycles to access the cubby hole where the lawn chairs Morilla ordered online were stored. I discovered unopened boxes stacked in the cargo hold that I'm sure we must have needed. Morilla ordered them, so I'm sure they'll come in handy, though I had no earthly idea as to their contents.

I arranged the lawn chairs under the awning in a straight row. I walked a few steps toward Buck's camper, then turned around for a look. With the Blue and White awning over the top of four folding chairs, and with the awning's trim edge flapping in the breeze, our patio looked like a grave side tent at a funeral. "Oh well," I said under my breath. "Morilla will fix it."

"Honey," I announced coming through the door, "I'm going to lay down for a nap. I don't even think she heard me. "Oh, Joe. I'm so glad we stopped here! I just love our new neighbors!" "Yea, me too," I said while kicking off my boots. She was still talking a blue streak as I cuddled up with the pups and drifted off.

"Joe?... Honey, It's almost dark. I thought you might want to wash up before we go next door." Sookie and Jazz hit the floor wagging their tails and soaking up Morilla's love. Nigel waited to see if I was going to roll out. "Hi, Baby," I said pulling her in for a kiss. You need to brush your teeth too Joe!" She said glancing off my lips with a butterfly kiss.

When my eyes focused, I could see that Morilla was dressed like an Island girl. She had a purple flower in her hair. I was later to find it had come from a flower bed outside the shower house. She had on a blue tie-died tee shirt with a peace sign in the middle. It was two sizes too large for her with a knot tied on one side. The knot hung down to the left pocket of her blue-jean shorts. "Cool!" I said... a hippie chic... How 'bout some of that "FREE LOVE, Baby?" "Maybe later lover boy!"

I washed my face, brushed my teeth, and popped the top on my first cold one of the day. Then I went outside to smoke. There was a cardboard box full of cardboard boxes. Morilla had decorated our patio. There was a string of festive lights strung around the parameter of the awning with great big colorful clothespins. Centered on the concrete patio, was a card table with four chairs around it.

They were the same chairs I'd unpacked earlier, but now they were fitted with cushions. There was a sunbathing chair all stretched out and comfortable looking. On the far end was a new Weber Bar-B-Que grill.

Morilla was hanging out the camper door smiling all over herself. "What cha' think Joe?" I snatched her up off the camper step and twirled her. "I think you've decorated my world far too long for me to ever live without you now, Morilla. I know I've got a funny last name and all... And people are gonna' make fun of you, just like they do me... That is... If you say yes to the question I've wanted to ask you for a long time now."

I set her down on her bare feet and humbled myself to one knee. "Morilla... will you marry me?" I held her hand and looked up with pleading eyes. She gazed down at me with all the love I could ever hope for. "Yes Joe, I'll marry you." I popped up and took her for another spin. "Morilla Pie. I say. Can you live with that?" I asked. "Sure! She says Laughing. I'll just change my first name to Peachie!"

CHAPTER

FOURTEEN

"Y'all 'bout ready?" Came a booming voice from across the way. It was Buck. "We'll be right there!" I hollered back. "Let me grab my sandals," Morilla says, scurrying into the camper. She came bouncing back down the steps. "I can't wait to tell Sadie!"

Morilla and Sadie evidently had a theme going. They both had flowers in their hair, but Sadie's was a vibrant Yellow. She wore a white denim skirt. The kind that Hippie chicks used to make out of blue jeans back in the day. Their flowers were identical except for the color. Both flowers had little tongues sticking out from the center of the bloom that bounced when the girls walked. They were both slim and attractive bottle Blondes. They were both quite sexy and girlish for their chronological age.

Buck and Sadie's patio was furnished much like ours,

except Buck had a bug zapper and a hammock. "Cool! I said. Ain't nothing like a bug zapper when your team loses, or your ole lady's pissed off, or you've drunk way too much. There are those times when the sound of a bug being zapped is enough to make you pump your fist in victory.

Sadie had a variety of Hummingbird feeders strung in various places. Morilla walked around the front yard discovering and admiring them like a kid finding Easter eggs. The care and feeding of Hummingbirds captured Morilla's attention as Sadie talked on the subject expounding with her hands in order to explain it more.

Locally sourced sea food aromas suffused the air as they tumbled together with wafts of Hickory smoke rising from Buck's carefully tended Bar-B-Q grill. I watched as he mopped sauces and buttery-flavored potions over bamboo skewers loaded with a variety of taste-tantalizing temp-tations.

Buck explained that flatbed trucks heavily laden with ice chests came through the park daily, selling what the locals called "The Catch of the Day." They will serve you, he explained, or you can serve yourself. "They even take credit cards." He added.

Peeled shrimp and buttery chunks of lobster. Grouper, pompano and mullet. Stone crab meat, and Spanish mackerel. A veritable feast punctuated with a variety of peppers and veggies and citrus and such. A meal fit for a King, not to be outdone except for the sparkling wine, and hospitality with which the dinner was served.

"Here's to our new friends, Joe and Morilla." Buck proclaimed. "Here Here!" Sadie saluted. The plastic wine glasses did not ring like fine Crystal, but neither did they subtract from the finery of our new friend's toast... "Bon Appetit!"

When the table was cleared, the dinner wine had been replaced by spirits containing a bit more gaiety. When the moon began to rise, the lonesome moan of a harmonica called in anguished tones from off in the distance. That's when neighbors and friends of neighbors, would bring glad tidings and ice chests full of their own choice of magical elixirs. They had come to celebrate this modern-day gypsy lifestyle each of them shared in common.

Some would bring cased instruments. Some, a guitar slung over their shoulder. Others with bongo drums or Cajons; or egg-shaped percussion instruments. Buck was the leader. He sat atop a bar stool on the patio slightly higher, and forward from his band of renowned. They sat on pickle buckets and ice chests resting instruments in their laps as Sadie waved the excited group to silence. With the countenance of a grand promoter, she elevated her voice: Ladies and Gentlemen... please give a big welcome to... "Buck Novocain... And The Deep Root Drillers!"

An energetic round of applause went up as Buck held his bow in an arched Calais style and counted off the band... 2) 3) 4). There they were... off and runnin' like a house afire!

Buck's traveling band was all dressed in white shirts with vents in the back. A style set aside for dentists, pharmacists, and chiropractors. Being as they were dentists who all wore dentures, they also shared a mantra in common: "Be True to your Teeth... or they'll be False to You!"

Buck would kick the whole thing off. Everyone would join in when they took a notion. All in all, they didn't sound half bad as each one Added his own layer to the impromptu music onion.

Mainly, everyone present felt like extended family in Buck's circle. Like they were a part of something. Even if that something was nothing more than a bunch of old folks hanging out, and having the time of their lives. Leonard Cohen said it best when he sang: "Like a bird, on the wire. Like a drunk, in some ole midnight choir. I have tried, in my way, to be free."

I was invited to participate several times that evening but engaged only a couple of times. "I'm happy just listening to y'all, and holding Morilla's hand," I said with a measured amount of fanfare. This got me big brownie points with Morilla. She and I sat exchanging the love-laced glances of a couple who had just become newly betrothed. Besides... I really didn't want to play. All I could think about was a gift Buck had given me... and getting Morilla home.

When the band was on their second break, Morilla and I mingled with our new neighbors. We shook hands and expressed our regret for leaving before we'd had our fill of such a fun-filled evening. Blaming our early departure on obligations beyond our control. After special thanks to Buck and Sadie, we said an all-around farewell to all and headed back to our own camp.

FIFTEEN

As we walked across the patch of grass between our patio and the Simmons', we noticed from that distance how merrily our string of party lights twinkled and danced around the awning's parameter. How they set off the overall look of the place. "The Gypsy Traveler... Ain't she a Beaut Morilla?" "I love her too Joe. I just wished we had a backyard to park her in. I hate to say it, Joe... But I'm homesick already. I miss checking the mail and having a bathtub. I want to hang Hummingbird feeders in our own yard. I don't want the hummingbirds to show up only to find us gone.

If we're going to get married, Joe. We need a home of our own. Not my house in Round Rock; or an apartment in New Orleans. If we're going to be married, we need a home of our own Joe. A yard where Sookie Nigel and Jazzy can run and play; and bury bones. A place of our own.... a place to call home, Joe."

Leading her onto the patio, I unlocked the door to let the pups out. We hadn't been gone for more than a few hours, but they were used to being under our feet 24/7. Which is just where we liked them!

Morilla's mood soon turned fanciful once she started talking about what a perfect couple we were, and how happy and carefree life would be once we found a cozy little home. Not too big, but not too small. One just large enough to contain all the happiness and joy we can fill it with." She punctuated her statement with a kiss "We don't need anything with an upstairs Joe." She continued. "I know it doesn't seem like it sometimes... but we're getting older Joe." To this, I responded. "You don't even look anywhere near old enough to retire Honey!" "Just look at ya.' Out here runnin' footloose and fancy-free! I bet people wonder why you're running with an old goat like me... I've seen them younger fellas checking your sweet ass out!"

Morilla has always gone to great lengths to keep her appearance youthful. Her hair would not be the Honey Gold color it is, were it not for a secret kept between her and her hairdresser. Nor would her lips be so plump and full if it wasn't for those occasional afternoons out with a girlfriend. On those occasions, she always shops for me. Morilla seems to think I won't notice that her lips look like they've been attacked by a whole hive of honeybees if I have a new guitar tuner to play with. I'm glad to know she has a bank account fat enough to support her exuberant extravagances. These things I consider all to my benefit. She endures the pain. I consume the pleasure.

"Morilla... Look at these. "I showed her a bubble pack of little "Blue" pills. "Joe," Morilla says in astonishment. "Where did they come from?" "Buck gave'em to me when he was showing me the Air Stream. When we were in the bathroom he said: "Hey Joe, you ever tried these? "I tell him, "no." He says: "Try some." Then he stuffs them in my shirt pocket." "You wanna' try some Morilla?" Says I. "Well... We did just get engaged," she said wistfully.

Earlier on, before I ask Morilla to marry me? I might have been obliged to expound on some of the kinkier, and most particularly fun parts of that night. How do we play "Rodeo" and all? But now that she and I are betrothed, it might not be decent. I'd hate to jump the "Holy" out of our "Matrimony," before we ever even find a preacher. All I can say is this: "If it can be tried, we tried it! If it can be done, we did it, and if we liked it, we did it twice!"

CHAPTER
SIXTEEN

Daybreak found us frolicking in the surf, still intoxicated by the love we'd found so late in our years. We were both aware that the day would come when we couldn't do this anymore. The very fact that; "That Day," had not yet arrived was reason enough for our all-night celebration. We walked the beach back to Pearl R.V. Park and slipped in The Gypsy Traveler uninterrupted by the park's (Early Birds.) All we wanted was sleep!

Around lunchtime, I awoke from a dream about my childhood. I was at my grandma's house in Rising Fawn, Georgia. I was on top of the chicken house watching my grandma feed the chickens. I could hear them pecking sporadically. Just about the time I was fixin' to jump off the chicken house with this big Black umbrella I used as a kid for a parachute, the smell of coffee stuck its fingers up my nose and drug me out of bed. Morilla was pecking at her laptop like a house afire. That must have been what brought on my dream about chickens.

She was so entranced in her work that she didn't even notice me until I kissed her on the neck. "Good morning, Sweetie!" "Good morning, Joe!" I've got a brand-new Idea for my next book." She said excitedly. "It's where this Gold digger woman forges this old man's will. Then she gives him Viagra and tries to screw him to death! What do you think Joe?" She asks with a mischievous grin.

"I think I'm glad you're the one with the money!" I said teasingly. "I ain't got a pot to piss in, or a window to throw it out of, but you liked to have screwed me to death anyway!" Few and far between were the days we didn't start with laughter. "Do you think it's a good premise, Joe?" "Hell yea, Baby... Just as long as I don't win the Lottery!

"Let me finish this paragraph, and I'll fix us some brunch... Anything you want in particular Joe?" "Whatever you feel like fixing Sweetheart... Long as it ain't Peachie Pie!" "Get your fill did ya'?" She asked laughing. Morilla poured me a steaming cup, then I took the dogs out for their long overdue morning duty. I sat under the awning and watched them sniff around in the green grass with Poop bags at the ready. The only real downside about having fur babies is the poop. I don't mind doggie pee, But... it irks my ass to no end when people don't clean up after their animal's #2 duty.

I remember one time when I was street corner pickin' down in New Orleans. (This was long before I met Morilla.) Jazz took a dump right there on the sidewalk. This particularly fancy lady was walking her dog past me just as ole Jazz was about to pinch one off. She turns to me and says: "I hope you're going to clean that up!" "Yes Mam! I always do!" says I.

With quickness, I grab a poop bag from my guitar case and scoop Jazz's poop. Then I ran to the trash can so she'd know that I did it. She and her dog are behind me now. When they catch up, her dog hikes his leg and pisses on the trashcan, then he shits like a Russian racehorse. I stare at her in total disgust. "I hope you're going to clean that up, Lady?" "Good morning, Joe." It's Sadie. She pulls me back from my dog poop daydream. "Is Morilla up and around?" I stick my head in the door. "Morilla... Sadie's here! "Morilla is at the door in three shakes. "Good morning, Sadie, she says jovially. Want some coffee?"

With both women chattering in gleeful tones, I shut the camper door and ventured off with the pups. They are eager to explore all the fresh scents that come with each new day. They sniff around until we finally end up at Buck's place, where he and I finish off the pot of coffee that Sadie had made earlier.

SEVENTEEN

Come to find out, Buck had always been just a broke assed musician like myself. Just like Morilla, it was Sadie who was loaded. Sadie is a jewelry broker. Buck used to work for Sadie and her husband selling jewelry in their main store. That's where they met and fell in love. Now they travel the country buying and selling precious metals and gems. She and her ex-husband are still business partners. He runs the brick-and-mortar stores, and she buys and sells online.

From the very beginning, me and Buck talked like we'd known each other all our lives. We were cut from the same cloth. Both of us would be lost if not for the women who had come along just in time to save us. We'd both fought for sobriety from the bandstand. The bandstand is a place where flamboyant drunkenness is not only tolerated but celebrated. Neither of us were teetotalers, but we weren't drunks anymore either.

Buck and I were deeply engrossed in a game of penny Annie poker when Morilla came running up. "Look, Joe!" Morilla held out her left hand with a wedding ring on her finger. It all but blinded me as it caught the sunlight. "Isn't it the most beautiful thing you've ever seen?" She asked. "I really, really want it, Joe!" She said bouncing on bare feet.

I put down my poker hand. "Morilla, I'll have to say that's a beautiful ring all right, but you know darn well I can't afford a rock like that, Honey!" "You can use my money to buy it, Joe! I'll loan it to you if you want. She offered. You can pay me back After we're married. You'll have plenty of money then!... Oh please Baby... pretty please!"

"How much money are we talking?" "Just a thousand dollars, Joe. Sadie's in the jewelry business. This ring retails for $7.300.00 She ogles the ring never taking her eyes off it. Her fingers were arched backward and spread wide. Each finger was like individually wrapped taffy candies.

"I'll give you what I can scrape up for "Earnest money." I told Sadie." But you'll have to wait until the third of the month when I get my check for the rest. I can give you three hundred now... Is that okay?" "That works for me, Joe." Said Sadie. "Promise me two things though." "What's that Sadie?" "Promise me you'll always take good care of that girl, and that you will never... Ever... Tell anyone what you paid for that ring!" "Thank you, Sadie! I know you gave us a bargain because Morilla wants it so bad. It's more than I can afford, but I can't afford, not to afford it!"

"Oh, Joe! Morilla chimes in. Thank you for feeling that way... I love you so much!"

EIGHTEEN

Morilla waited longingly but patiently until the third of the month came. When it did, I went to an A.T.M. And emptied out my account leaving only the required five dollars to keep the account open. That afternoon I paid Sadie what I owed her on Morilla's ring. After a late lunch with the Simmons', we packed everything up and unhooked the water hose and septic system. We rolled up the awning and retracted the automatic leveling system. After hugs and handshakes and kisses were shared all 'round. We headed north on U.S. Highway One.

We hit the turnoff to Big Pine Key Just as the sun was about to sink into the ocean. "Let's stop in Big Pine Joe... There's something I want to do." "Now Morilla, you're just gonna' have to face it. We're gonna have to cross the Seven

Mile Bridge. There ain't no way around it!" "I know Joe… But there's something I want to do first please."

I made the turn on Big Pine Road and drove the posted speed limit. "And what might that be Honey?" I ask inquisitively. "I want to know what it feels like to make love with my wedding ring on… Just in case something was to happen." "Something like what? "I asked. "Something like going off that damn bridge!" Morilla whined tearfully. "Oh, Hell Honey!" Okay…

Morilla cuddled over close and took my hand. "Joe, I want to do it in the forestry tower." "The forestry tower? Are you out of your mind? Why if Barney Fife was to catch us screwing up there, they'd put us under the jail!" "They didn't put you and Janie in jail, did they?" "Well no. But that was a long time ago, Morilla. A lot's changed since then!" "So… You'd take the chance for Janie, but you won't take the chance for me?" I knew instantly when she said that, for me, this was a "No-win situation." The proverbial… damned if you do… and damned if you don't!"

I parked on the far side of the road from the forestry tower and popped the hood.

Then I pulled the coil wire out of the distributor so the R.V. Wouldn't start; just in case Barney showed up. That way we would have some kind of an excuse for being in the park. A reason besides my Morilla wanting to get fucked with her wedding ring on in the forestry tower.

I put out the necessary reflectors in front and back of

the coach. "Come on Morilla," I said with my hand stretched toward her. "You got my ring, Joe?" "It's in my pocket, Honey... You bring a pillow?" "No," Morilla said shortly. "If Janie could bare ass it... Then I can too!"

We climbed the stairway that zigzagged back and forth to the tower observatory deck where we caught our breath. Then took in a sight that had been frozen in time for me. Nothing had changed. It was still just as beautiful as it was, when Janie and I smoked joints up there, drink Strawberry Hill, and screwed our brains out!

"I can't believe how high this tower is Joe. It looks tall from the ground, but not this tall!" "The sign used to say 120 feet. But it seems like a mile; doesn't it Honey?"

We sat dangling our feet and holding on to the handrails talking in low tones for a while. "Will you put the ring on my finger now Joe? Then you can kiss the Bride."

Morilla said seductively.

Sex is something neither of us like to rush, but we both knew the longer we took, the better our chances were of getting caught. "Come on Baby... Let's get down to the main attraction!" Twenty minutes later, we were lumbering down the steps more breathless at the bottom, than when we'd first reached the top. "Damn the luck!" I say, killing my flashlight at the same time. There it was. The same old Fish and Wildlife cruiser rolling up. Blue lights flashing.

"Fricking Barney! That fool could screw up a wet

dream," I say under my breath. "What do we do now?" Morilla asks. "Stay low... and follow me." We go behind the tower over to the bushes and lurk in the shadows until we come to the road, then we cross the road and hope he doesn't see us. We acted like we were relieved to see the Ranger. As he approached, Morilla whispered... thank God it isn't Barney!

"I'm glad you happened along officer. I'm afraid we may need some help." I say in a thankful voice. "Having trouble are you?" The Ranger offered cordially. "Yeah." says I... "she just up and quit on us. I was lucky to get her off the road as far as I did." I handed Morilla the keys. "Try it again Honey." Morilla cranked on it hard, but it just wouldn't start. I'm shining the light on the motor while Morilla cranks and the Ranger looks on with me.

"There's your trouble Sir!" Says the Ranger. "The ignition coil wire has fallen off. "Mam. Turn your key to the "Off" position, please. He further instructs Morilla." "Don't touch that key! I'm going to stick my hand in close to the fan, Mam." He explains. "Okay, Officer," Morilla replies. The Ranger reaches down and plugs the coil wire back into the distributor.

"Stand clear." The Ranger says with the authority of a mechanic. "Try it now Mam." Morilla hits the key and sure enough, the Gypsy Traveler fires right up. The Ranger swipes his hands together like there wasn't nothin' to it. Then I grab his hand and shake it hard while offering up a most humble appreciation. Morilla hands him a paper towel, then reaches in for a hug. He accepts her hug like the Hero we'd convinced him he surely must be...

"Y'all be safe now, and watch for the deer," he says swaggering back toward his patrol car. I grab the reflectors while Morilla slides over to the passenger's seat. I jump in behind the wheel. We look at each other with a shit-eatin' grin and say in unison; "Wow... That was close!"

Feeling lucky as a Chimney Sweep, I take a left back onto U.S. Highway One toward Marathon. We're headed across the Seven Mile Bridge. I hear the R.V.'s bathroom door slam just as the lights of Marathon come into view. Morilla had been hiding in the bathroom while I drove across the bridge... or so I assumed. "Oh shit, she said in astonishment. "I forgot we had to cross the bridge!" "You weren't hiding in the bathroom?" I asked. "No," she said timidly. Well, what were you doing?" She laughed as we bumped off the bridge apron, and onto the island of Marathon. "I was pulling a splinter out of my butt."

CHAPTER
NINETEEN

Once we got back to the mainland, we headed the Gypsie Traveler toward Georgia. Our destination was Rising Fawn... not but three miles from the Tennessee line. Even though I was raised on those muddy banks, Morilla had never even seen the Tennessee River. She wanted us to buy a home where at least one of us was familiar with the surrounding area. The only place she'd ever been, was Oklahoma and Texas. I'd been coast to coast. From sea to shining sea. I'd been everywhere an ole Singing Cowboy can go on a song and a prayer. I'd seen it all... everything but... "The Big Time!"

Morilla had the Wedding Bell Blues something awful! She didn't even care about flirting with the truckers on the C.B. anymore. She'd searched for a place on the internet where she wanted to get married. She said it was "The place." It just so happened to be in Rising Fawn Georgia, where I was raised by my grandma. A place called, "Chapel in The Pines."

After I put that ring on her finger at the forestry tower on Big Pine? She ain't taken it off since. The way she goes on about getting married... And us buying a home? Why Hell! If we weren't so old, and I didn't know better... I'd think she was in a delicate way!

I'd overheard her talking to a real estate agent in Round Rock before we left the R.V. Park. "The key is under the door mat... she told him. Sure you can... I don't care! Tell them to make an offer! Look, Charlie... Just sell the damn thing!

Once Morilla made up her mind... Her mind was made up! When she sets out to do a thing... Ain't long before dust settles on it!

"Chapel In the Pines," was all she'd hoped it would be. She took her wedding ring off only one time since the forestry tower. That was so I could put it back on her again at the Altar.

The couples waiting in line behind us threw rice as we left as husband and wife. Just as we had done for the couples in front of us.

Morilla fell in love with Rising Fawn. We found a home there that seemed to be made just for us. It wasn't too far from Grandma's old home place. Sookie Nigel and Jazzy had a fenced-in yard in which to play. And a place to bury their bones. The house was not too big or too small. It was just what we wanted. Just big enough to hold all the love we could pile in it.

Morilla and I made only one trip to Round Rock, Texas after that. We flew down to close on her house, then we rented a U-Hall to move her keepsakes and an antique bedroom suit her grandmother had given her as a house-warming gift when she bought the house in Round Rock some 40 years ago.

Much like she did in New Orleans. A parade of delivery trucks showed up with whatever she'd ordered online. In a couple of weeks, even the dogs knew... We were home!

Looking back now, I can see how Morilla thought she wanted to travel. I can see how the life I led while she was educating herself for a prosperous career, then educating herself thereafter on each year's new tax laws, had placed a heavy burden on her. I can see now how she fell for a near-do-well like myself. Her life had been spent in a velvet cage. Mine was cast iron. Now I see why Angels fall in love with outlaws.

It was there in Rising Fawn that Morilla began to write. I mean... Really write!

Rarely did I look in her eyes and not see a storyline that had consumed her. Sex was my only way in... and her only way out. Ravenous sex, like starving wolves gorging them-selves in moonlight shadows.

I had lost my Morilla... not to another lover, but to her

craft. The lights in her study burned nightly while I lay alone waiting for dawn to come. Her pillow on our bed lay plump in the morning sun. As though it were a testament to her dedication.

Mornings would oftentimes find me in the garden outside her plate glass window staring up from the tulips she planted that first Spring. I'd lose track of time staring at the only woman in this lifetime, I would ever truly adore.

Many are the publications, and adorations her works had inspired. But none held a candle to what would be her best, and final work. It was in a fit of Murder Mystery Genius that she wrote. "When Dead Men Talk."

Friends began to call in sightings: "There are Media trucks at the Donut shop this morning." Free-lance photographers were becoming as common as Gray squirrels. When she made the New York Times Best Sellers List. Our private life was gone... Morilla Kaye Montgomery was a full-blown celebrity!

It was this White-hot heat of passion for her work that would take her from us all. It would take her from the flower gardens she tended between loving me and our dogs. The lawnmower she loved to ride. Her passion brought her to me... then took her from me... From our fur babies... from her readers... and eventually... from this world.

CHAPTER

TWENTY

"Joe! Wake up Joe." As my eyes drew up to a focus. I zoomed in on Morilla. It was her, right? But she looked different. She looked like all those "fancy folks" who stared at me when the dogs and I first walked into the lobby of the Ritz Carlton. Not only was She rich... she looked rich! After all the interviews and Press releases... T.V. shows and talk radio, I was finally coming to terms with the fact that my wife was not only rich... but she was famous too!

I noticed people all dressed in finery like Morilla were anxiously milling around when a lady holding a clipboard to her bosom said: "Everyone follow me please." She led a troop of people through the large, cased opening that led to the plush meeting room I'd only poked my head into earlier.

"You look like a Movie Star Morilla." "Thank you, Joe... This is how they want me to look for my debut on "Good Morning America." Everyone is here from the show to tighten up a few loose ends before tomorrow's broadcast. I want you to be on your best behavior Joe. There are a lot of important people here tonight. People who are important to my career... and our future. Wiping the sleep from my eyes, I rise up and kiss Morilla... Even her lips are different... Round and hard as a new steel belted radial. She even smells different.

Just about that time a short knock comes at the door. A tall thin man dressed in tails lets himself right on in. Then he hollers... "Make way!" He holds the door as a silver-wheeled cart is pushed in with a whole string of workers dressed like chefs making their way to the conference room.

Me, I'm slipping on my shit, kikkers. Morilla comes up off the side of the bed and goes to greet him. The dogs are about like me, they don't know what to make of it all. The hair on Nigel's neck is raised like a porcupine. Ain't nobody gonna get that squirrel tail! I leash up the dogs and check my pocket for the hotel key. Nigel grabs his squirrel tail, and the three of us head down the hall and make for the elevator.

TWENTY-ONE

We spend more time in New York City than we do at home anymore. There's a new lady behind the check-in desk this trip. I don't think she likes me much, so I try not to draw her disapproving eye, but it seems I always do. It's easy to see that she doesn't like my kind.

Fresh air hits us at the front door. Fresh as you can hope to find in this God-forsaken rat hole. Me and the pups spend most of our time outside when we're at the Ritz. The air doesn't smell like home. It smells like subway trains and taxicabs.

We cross at the light and head over into Central Park, then head for the nearest grove of trees with a park bench. Jazzy and Sookie make a break for their freedom when I drop their leashes. Nigel usually does too, but this time he lays at my feet gnawing on his squirrel tail. It's quickly becoming worse for the ware. I light a smoke and think about the life we had, and how much has changed since Morilla hit the "Big Time."

I think about ole "Novocain Buck and The Deep Root Drillers." He and Sadie. They were two peas in a pod if ever there was. I'll never forget those two. I think about my old landlord James, and how he's doing with the Air B&B. About how Morilla had first created it for us, then gifted it to him after we bought the Gypsie Traveler. Most of all, I think about the carefree woman Morilla used to be. Back when all she wanted to do was make music on Royal Street in the daytime and make love to me at night. How she was jealous of the forestry tower. How she wanted my last memory of it to be shared with her, and not Janie.

I sat on the park bench missing home, and waiting for New York City's rush hour traffic to be over. For the impatient drivers to quit honking their horns. For the constant stream of people to finally find their way home. After our first few trips to the Big Apple, I realized... they never would.

I gathered up the kids and headed back to the Ritz. I noticed on my way up to the 33rd floor that the squeaking elevator pulley had still been denied what it obviously needed from the very first time I rode it...All it needed was a few pumps of grease.

TWENTY-TWO

People were huddled in clusters around the water feature as I made my way to our Suite. Cameras flashed, while grips held blue screens, and spotlights mixed with those in the fountain's sprays. It was Morilla. She was dressed differently now.

Three boom mics hung just above the tan velvet couch where she sat between her Agent Joe Bartello and Tiffany Wise as the cameras rolled. Tiffany's face was unmistakable. Hers was a household name. She was the host of Good Morning America. I stood there in awe of this elegant beauty that I'd made my wife. Morilla was dressed in Sea Spray Green. The lights, like a teenage gang bang, all took a turn at her. Oddly dressed as I was in comparison, no one seemed to notice me, so I slipped down the hall past Norman Rockwell's paintings.

What once seemed extravagant on our first stay at the Ritz, had become plain compared to what Morilla had apparently become accustomed to. Me and the dogs headed toward room 333 which had become our temporary home here in New York City.

I opened our door and followed my nose straight into the conference room. It looked like a ballroom now. No one except for the bartender and food servers were there. With an amazing sense of timing, the food servers took their places and lifted the silver domes away from the steam table revealing before me, a virtual smorgasbord of culinary delights. Just everything you can imagine!

The staff treated us with an extraordinary level of hospitality. Even the dogs were tended. Nigel dropped his squirrel tail, opting for a selection of bacon-wrapped quail breasts and leg of lamb sauteed in a flagrant cream sauce.

"What's your poison?' Asks the bartender from the far end of the conference room. "I'll have a tall glass of milk for now." Says I. Jazz and Sookie followed me as slices of savory roast beef and other delicacies were generously piled on our plates. We followed Nigel and his server back to the bedroom, where we ate like cavemen who had just invented fire.

After dinner, the dogs stretched. All three of them piled up in the bed this time. Nigel seemed to be glad the squirrel tail was gone, and that he was back at the center of his harem.

I bellied up to the bar and asked the bartender if he could make a White Russian out of the milk left in my glass. He went into a bottle-flipping routine that soon revealed the delightful elixir at my request. The service crew seemed to be at ease while maintaining a certain level of professionalism.

They all came to attention as Tiffany Wise and Morilla came strolling in escorted by Joe Bartello. They were seated first by a smartly dressed woman in a satin blouse and Black skirt. Then came an elegant glide path of production elites who were seated at evenly spaced tables surrounding the table where Morilla was seated. The rows of tables further back were for the camera crew, dolly grips, sound men, and technical people who were known for their expertise, but not for their political or social standing in the media hierarchy.

I tipped my hat to the ladies as I made my way out of the conference room. I stood just outside the door with my White Russian hoping beyond hope, that I wasn't an embarrassment to Morilla.

When everyone was seated, a large Sterling tray was placed in the center of the room on a sturdy folding base. Through the cased doorway, a precision team of glass handlers stacked wine glasses in a pyramid whose height demanded the assistance of a platform ladder. When the task was complete, the glass handlers fell in formation and exited the conference room with the same synchronized expedience. Simultaneously, the tall thin man in tales stood atop the platform later and addressed all in attendance. He held his arms wide and began to speak.

"Ladies and gentlemen. As I'm sure you all know, we are here tonight to celebrate the accomplishments of Mrs. Morilla Kaye Montgomery. (Everyone began to clap, and continued to do so until Joe Bartello lent his hand to Morilla, helping her to her feet and presenting her to the master of ceremonies.)

The tall thin man in tails received her hand, then continued to speak. "Mystery is one of the most popular genres out there. It is also one of the most competitive. From out of nowhere came this beautiful mysterious woman whose work would in a short span of time land her titles consistently on the New York Times Best Sellers List.

Many aspire to those lofty heights. Almost as many... come away disappointed.

Morilla Kaye Montgomery's last release has set the publishing world on its literary ear!" "When Dead Men Talk," has sat at the very pinnacle of the mystery genre selling on par with authors who have written their names indelibly in the American consciousness. Names like Daniel Nathan, Emanuel Benjamin, P.D. James, and Agatha Christie."

The pop of champagne corks fills the air as the tall man in Tales pours the top glass full. It overflows into the two below it. They overflow into the three below them and so on until the pyramid of champagne glasses shimmers and shines in a frosty effervescent show of Spirits.

Morilla receives the glass on top, and then everyone else in the group is served.

"To Morilla Kaye Montgomery... When Dead Men Talk!" Says the tall thin man in tales. Glasses go up... "Cheers!" Everyone shouts in unison. They pay homage to Morilla and congratulate her on her "Book of the Year award. Then they grab a plate and join the smorgasbord line.

One old lady stands in the far corner of the room. She looks sullen like a broody ole hen with her pin feathers ruffled. She is as square-jawed as Sargent Carter and rotund as Jackie Gleason. "Oh, Hell no!" I say to myself. "It's the fat lady with the Poodle dog who wanted Nigel's squirrel tail!

I ease my way through the schmoozing circle and catch Morilla around the waste. "Congratulations Honey!" I say, stealing her away greedily from the center of the circle. "I've never seen you look so pretty, Morilla." I kiss her neck to remind myself that no matter how famous she has become, that privilege is still mine.

As we walk toward the balcony, I point out the fat lady, who is still standing in the corner sulking. "Who is that old battle ax Morilla?" Morilla holds her hand to her mouth in order to hide a snicker. "Walk me out to the balcony Joe, and I'll tell you."

I stroll Morilla like she is my prom queen through the double glass sliding doors out to the balcony. "That's Beatrice Tully. She's an amazing writer, one of my favorites." "So that's her?... I've seen her books in your study." I said. "You know Morilla, her Poodle dog tried to take Nigel's squirrel tale down in the lobby when we checked in this afternoon. Nigel didn't give it up though." "Where'd Nigel get a squirrel's tale?" Morilla asked with a curious smile. "In Central Park. I'll tell you all about it when you see his nose." Says I. "No wonder Bernice is so pissed!" Morilla exclaimed. "I got the New York Times Book of the Year, and my dog snubbed her dog." Morilla giggled.

We stood in the cool night air looking out over the city. We were high above the noise. Only the sound of horns honking and police sirens could be heard from below. Skyscrapers and flashing lights were visible as far as the eye could see. Cars with headlights aglow moved slowly through a grid of intersections that grew smaller and smaller in the distance, until the roads and the cars they carried, dropped off the edge of the world.

"Oh, Joe... This is no life for us Honey! It's all just too much! After this is all over, I want us to go out in the motor home again. I've done what I wanted to do. I'm at the top of the heap now Joe. I know I've neglected you. I want to make it up to you Joe. I never knew my writing career would turn out like this. I want our simple life back. Just you and me and Nigel and Sookie and Jazzy! We were so happy back then Honey!... Everything was so easy!"

"Do you really mean it Morilla? You have a mailbox now. The kids have a place to play and bury their bones. We have a place to park the R.V. In the backyard now. I start the motor every day when we're home, just so I know the ole Gypsy Traveler is ready to go, should your passion for writing ever turn back into your passion for loving me and the Pup ups. Maybe we can catch up to Buck and Sadie again! Oh, Morilla... I love you so much, Honey!"

"I mean it, Joe. Writing has taken more away from me than I would have ever given it, had I known then, what I know now. Work has always given me everything I thought I wanted... Now that I have everything I ever wanted, I'm not going to work anymore. Love and youth are the two most beautiful things in life. I can't regain my youth, but I can give all my love to you from now on Joe Pie. As long as you and I are together Honey. I'll never ask for anything more."

"Pardon me Morilla." It's Joe Bartello. He glances at me with a dismissive look.

Before he has a chance to dominate the conversation, I pull her in for a smack on the lips. "I'm gonna go smoke Honey." On my departure, our fingers brushed for the last time.

I used to feel guilty when I thought about it. There are always so many (What-ifs when fate turns on a dime.

What if I'd led her back from the railing? What if I'd told Joe Bartello that Morilla wasn't feeling well, and whatever he wanted with her would just have to wait? What if's goes on forever until you realize that the inevitable always happens anyway and that the price of living... is dying?

I was smoking a cowboy killer in front of the Ritz, talking to one of the doormen when it happened. We both heard the screams. "Must be another jumper! Ain't no wonder this place is so damned haunted!" He exclaimed. Fifty yards away we heard the impact. "Rich folks ain't never happy." He said matter of factly. "The more they get... The more they want. I don't know why they insist on making a mess on the sidewalk damn their asses! It's mostly famous folks ya' know?" He added.

"Well, time for me to punch out." He says looking at his watch. "Don't guess I'll be walking that way tonight, no Sir!' Ever seen what a mess a body makes? Don't trouble yourself with lookin'. It ain't nothin' nice!"

Sirens whale in the distance, as I toss my cigarette butt and walk through the lobby toward the elevator. The cables strained even harder than they had earlier. The pulley which had only squeaked before, began to beg for mercy.

The elevator ground to a grueling halt on the 27th floor. The double doors opened, and the old Black Captain who tended the 33rd floor was standing in the elevator doorway. "Oh... It's you!" He said, stepping inside with his wheelcart.

The scowl on his face told me he was disgusted that the most he could ever get out of me was a ten-dollar tip. "Going up?" I asked. "I'm going down!" He retorted sharply, slapping the ground floor button simultaneously!

He was going down alright! We both were! The elevator cables squalled furiously! The elevator jerked and rose a few feet... Then dropped like a rock! I only rode one roller coaster in my life, that's because this girl in junior high called me a chicken. If it weren't for that day, I would have no way of telling you what it sounded like. Or.... What it felt like! You know how it sounds when you fall off the top and you're picking up speed? How does it feel when the world falls out from underneath you? Like that!

The first thing I remember hearing was the ole Captain's voice. He was laughing! The first thing I remember seeing was the ole Captain. He was dragging himself out of his body. (What there was left of it!) He was Black and I was White but the mess we made when we hit just all oozed together like eggs when you put'em in a bowl and take a fork to them. "Well by God ole Betsy finally broke!" That's what the captain kept saying over and over. "Well by God... Ole Betsy finally broke!"

We both hovered up by the sealing in the elevator for a long time just looking down at our bodies. "I can't tell you from me," I say. "Can you tell me from you?" "Not so as ta' speak of." He says quizzically. "One thing I do know." He adds emphatically. "I know that little pea shooter of a pecker over there in the corner must be yours, 'cause it ain't mine!" The old Black man says laughing hardily. "Yea... Well, I'll throw dicks with you any day!" Says I. "I'll take you up on that! The ole Captain says. "Yea well" ... Says I... "You gotta find yours first!" Now were both laughing!

While the fire department is scooping us up with snow shovels and puking all over us, a swirl of wind catches us both up and sets us side by side in the lobby. There we are attended by an Angel. I know it sounds crazy, but the dude was ten feet tall and had wings and silk robes and a Halo and shit! If it quacks like a duck or walks like a duck?... Trust me! This dude was an Angel!

CHAPTER

TWENTY-THREE

You would think that when you cross over from one life to the next it will all be like divine and stuff. Right? ... A person would think that once you're dead, you've seen the last of paperwork, right?... Wrong! The Angel handed us both a clipboard. It said: "Welcome to Purgatory!"

The check yes or no boxes were as would be expected, but the script was written in a language that was alien to me. What was really strange is, I could read it! The skinny of it was that "Yes" ... There is a God. And that in time you would stand in judgment for sins. That you would be graded on a curve that takes into consideration the sins of your father and all the wild shit you did from puberty through college.

Usually, it's the small print in every document I've ever

signed that got me screwed. (Heaven must have some great lawyers!) Just above the signature line; a paragraph read as follows: You were born of sin. It is on that sin that you will be judged. Until then... Enjoy Purgatory!

I read the whole thing over again just to make sure my eyes weren't playing tricks on me. Sure enough, I can sin here in purgatory all I want, and it won't count against me. I signed on the dotted line and turned to the Captain. "You thinkin' what I'm thinkin'?" You thinkin' 'bout goin' to the Bar?" He axed. Yes indeedie! Says I.

"I'll get the first round," says he... bring you such a tight ass nigga! We both busted out!

Well... sitting right there at the bar still in her Winter Green dress was Morilla. She wasn't any September Rose anymore... She was fresh as a Daisy, and juicy as the pistol from the center of a honeysuckle. Morilla Kaye Montgomery was settin' right there... Slap dab in the best days of her prime!

I wasn't all that sorry to hear that the fat lady with the Poodle dog was so upset about not winning the New York Times Best Selling Book of The Year award, that she committed suicide, but I was sorry that she pulled Morilla over the handrail with her. Morilla was mostly upset that Beatrice Tully hit a tree, and that her body was in one piece mostly. Morilla said she hit so hard that she turned to mush. It was obvious that she was still pissed about it too!

Time goes kind of funny when you're in purgatory.

Nobody wears a watch. Time ain't nothing because time isn't linear anymore. Over what you still probably count as time, Morilla has grown very fond of Hugh Hefner. As for me, I've never found anything more enticing than Liz Taylor... and her Baby Doll Pajamas!

THE END